'This is a hold-up.
Fill this balloon with gas'

THE BEST OF
MATT
2009

MATTHEW PRITCHETT

studied at St Martin's School of Art in London and first saw himself published in the *New Statesman* during one of its rare lapses from high seriousness. He has been the *Daily Telegraph*'s front-page pocket cartoonist since 1988. In 1995, 1996, 1999 and 2005 he was the winner of the Cartoon Arts Trust Award and in 1991, 2004 and 2006 he was 'What the Papers Say' Cartoonist of the Year. In 1996, 1998, 2000, 2008 and 2009 he was the *UK Press Gazette* Cartoonist of the Year and in 2002 he received an MBE.

Own your favourite Matt cartoons. Browse the full range of Matt cartoons and buy online at www.telegraph.co.uk/photographs or call 020 7931 2076.

'That was the day
someone bought a
plastic carrier bag'

The Daily Telegraph

THE BEST OF

MATT

2009

An Orion paperback

First published in Great Britain in 2009 by
Orion Books
A division of the Orion Publishing Group Ltd
Orion House
5 Upper St Martin's Lane
London WC2H 9EA

An Hachette UK company

10 9 8 7 6 5 4 3 2 1

A CIP catalogue record for this book
is available from the British Library

ISBN 978 1 4091 0364 6

Printed in the UK by CPI William Clowes, Beccles NR34 7TL

The Orion Publishing Group's policy is to use papers that
are natural, renewable and recyclable products and
made from wood grown in sustainable forests. The logging
and manufacturing processes are expected to conform to
the environmental regulations of the country of origin.

www.orionbooks.co.uk

MY FAVOURITE

MATT

CARTOON

My Favourite Matt Cartoon

The four most depressing words are 'Matt is on holiday'. Creativity versus Bureaucracy – the genius of Matt.

Richard Briers

'I shall now attempt
to fail a GCSE'

You could choose the best cartoon by randomly opening a page and stabbing down your finger. Matt never fails. He is one of the few people living and working in Britain today who never has an off day. They say 'even Homer nods', well Matt never nods. And on top of that his cartoons are never mean-spirited, cruel or pleased with themselves.

Stephen Fry

My Favourite Matt Cartoon

'WAIT! . . . I can make
RoboDog wave goodbye'

Matt's wonderfully funny, exquisitely drawn cartoons bring a light to the darkest day. But I was really upset by the cartoon in which RoboDog was installed in the house and stood on the doorstep waving goodbye to the family dog. I rang up Matt and said I was so sad about the family dog's plight. Within 24 hours he had drawn me a gorgeous sequel of the family dog thrusting RoboDog into the dustbin: a truly happy ending and terribly funny.

Jilly Cooper

'Your card is fine.
I'm just checking that your
bank hasn't expired'

When we were all slitting our throats over the financial crisis and inveighing against the banks, Matt made us absolutely scream with laughter. As a scatty geriatric I always panic that there won't be any money in my account, or I've put in the wrong PIN number. In this cartoon you can imagine the relief on the customer's face when the shop lady says she's checking on the bank rather than the customer – so brilliant. I Photostatted the drawing and sent it to all my friends who loved it equally.

Jilly Cooper

'I've got my own recovery plan. I'm asking Madonna to adopt me'

My slavish admiration of every Matt cartoon ever drawn is well known. Being asked to pick a favourite is like being asked to take my choice of the Crown Jewels. Every one a gem in the diadem of Matt's genius.

Sir Terry Wogan

As always, it's Matt's ability to take a complex issue and render it funny by normalising everything.

Jeremy Clarkson

THE BEST OF

MATT

2009

'As soon as I saw what I'd been up to, I knew the Speaker had to go'

'I'm going to cancel the papers if you go through the roof every morning'

MPs Expenses

'One day, son, all this
will be on expenses'

'I'm your local MP and
I've come to sneer at your
ghastly little house'

'Actually, for financial
reasons, I call this
my second home'

'Vote for me... I think I have a
house somewhere round here'

MPs Expenses

'Douglas Hogg has returned
some of his moat'

'Do you think we could fit
a plasma TV in there?'

'I'm only a Premiership footballer, love. You spend money like I'm an MP'

'If you put a copy of the Telegraph in the window it keeps the politicians away'

'My MP has a better washing machine than your MP'

'Nobody thanks us for keeping the retail sector going through this recession'

'I got a job here because I've always been interested in politics'

'We're scrapping ID cards. We don't want anyone to know we're MPs'

'Can you tell the fees office
I'm designating this as my
main residence?'

'HAPPY NOW?'

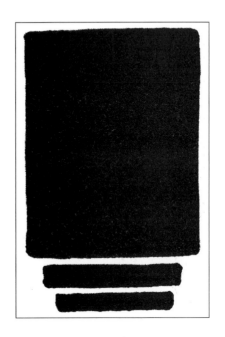

Redacted Matt

Labour Turmoil

'Don't take this as a criticism, but you're lamentable and I'm ashamed to be associated with you'

'I'm starting to miss the BBC's business editor, Robert Peston'

'Is there still a Labour party?'

'I think I'll push off now as well...'

EU Elections . . .

. . . and resignations

Labour Turmoil

'To cheer Gordon up I've
had all Labour's
Euro votes framed'

'If this is some sort of
loyalty test I'm not
taking part'

'I'm a banker. Give my bill
to one of the other tables'

'Don't ask for a
cash withdrawal'

Banks in trouble

'My dad's bank lost more money than your dad's bank'

'And that's, basically, how short-selling works'

'BUY SHARES IN CARDBOARD BOXES'

'This is my share of Lloyds TSB'

Redundancies

Credit Crunch

'Just give us your
******* money'

'I'm a taxpayer. How would
you like the money –
twenties or fifties?'

Bail-outs and bank help

'Mr Darling isn't here. It looks like he's making a statement at the moment'

'There are no tea bags left. We're staring into the abyss'

Things get even worse

'If the situation gets any
worse, Britain could
run out of zeros'

'I used to be superstitious,
but frankly, what else
can go wrong?'

The numbers get bigger

The debt mounts

Credit Crunch

'Don't pass those on to
the customers'

'Let's do something really
Christmassy – let's go and
live in a stable'

Banks stop lending

'Don't save money, son.
I advise gambling, loose
women and strong liquor'

'The grandchildren are here.
You distract them while I
steal their pocket money'

'For the first time the pound reached parity with a chocolate coin covered in foil'

'Let's sell up in the UK, go to France and buy a croissant'

Credit Crunch

'Is it possible to be alarmed and bored at the same time?'

'Get the Rolls out of the garage, Jenkins. I want you to run me over'

Credit Crunch

Treasury accused of being over-optimistic

The bonuses continue

'Avoid thinking about Sir Fred Goodwin – I see you've been grinding your teeth'

Call-out charge £30.
Glass £34.
Labour £52.
Bonus £7m.

Sir Fred tops unpopularity list . . .

. . . and his home is attacked

Credit Crunch

'I didn't get you a Mother's
Day present in case it was
seen as a reward for failure'

'I'm just so worried he'll
end up as a failed banker
with a £17m pension'

Spending Cuts

'I don't want any cuts. Just make sensible efficiencies and tough decisions'

'There won't be a spending review because we've decided it's vulgar to discuss money'

'There's a closing down
sale on Earth'

Retail Woes

'We don't lend money, but we have just taken over the pick 'n' mix business from Woolworths'

'Welcome to the store. Are you returning something or have you just come in to use the loo?'

'Only buy gifts from shops that will still be in business when I exchange them'

Car Industry

'You're in charge now'

'Will you sponsor me?
I'm going to sit in a bath of
baked beans to raise money
for the British car industry'

'I tell you what I miss – the smell of a brand-new car'

'Maybe we should halt production for a while'

Car Industry

'It doesn't need a tax disc
and it uses no fuel'

'I'm from the estate agent
next door. I just felt like
some company'

'Has it been on the
market long?'

'Cheer up, darlin''

'Your pocket money is for
sweets – you weren't
meant to buy a house'

'Will you take the
doll's house out of my room?
I'm having nightmares
about negative equity'

'We should move the demo forward. Capitalism may not last till next Wednesday'

'I can't get to London for the riots'

Anti-capitalist Riots

'On Wednesday I'm going to wear a pinstripe suit and walk through the City'

'May I just say what an excellent disguise that is, Chairman'

'I'll always remember where
I was when I slept through
the result'

'…and the whole world
lived happily ever after'

Obama wins

Obama

'They wouldn't serve me. They were too busy watching the inauguration'

RACE TO BE OBAMA'S PUPPY

'Can we fetch sticks? Yes we can'

Obama arrives at the White House

'Right, that's enough hope, I'm off to work'

Olympics

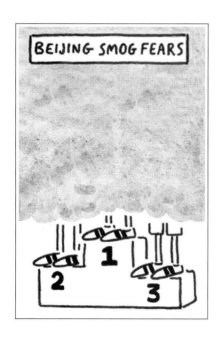

'I had to stop watching the Olympics – I'm sick of hearing the National Anthem'

'Who sent Team GB through the metal detector?'

Surprising success

Schools

'Well, anyway… it's a
new personal best'

'Tell me about when you
failed your exams in
the olden days'

'I've marked it myself'

'I was wrong – the waiting wasn't the worst part'

Exam chaos

'Before I declare my undying love, which airline is your return ticket booked with?'

Airlines go bust

'For a few worrying hours
I could hear every word my
wife said to me'

Strikes . . .

'Ladies and gentlemen,
the oxygen masks have
dropped down. A stewardess
will be along shortly
to charge you for them'

. . . and budget airlines

Where to land a plane

'I've only got a bad back, but I've emptied your waiting room'

Swine flu arrives from Mexico

'Apparently, the Government has only enough swine flu medicine for half the population'

'We want our son to go to a school with swine flu. The local comprehensive only has nits'

'I won't panic until the Government says it has everything under control'

'That whale is in our
garden again'

Snow

'There's a £2 gas surcharge
if you want your
steak well done'

'Merde!'

Royal Mail

'Privatised mail: We tried to deliver a package today. Please go to our depot in Holland to collect it'

'Our names were in a prize draw and we've won the Royal Mail'

'This is a message for Dr Who: I slept with your vacuum cleaner'

'I wish you'd be a little less edgy and contemporary'

Jonathan Ross

Teenage Parents

'I had a maths test today
and tomorrow I've got
a paternity test'

'It's not truancy, I'm on
paternity leave'

Strictly Come Dancing

'Have you been seeing John Sergeant?'

'I'm worried that John Sergeant's dancing is driving down the value of the £'

'I'm having my doubts about
these low-energy light bulbs'

'One advantage of these
low-energy bulbs is that
there's not enough light to
read my gas bill'

'Is this a government health warning about middle-class drinking?'

'The geese have flown.'
'And the squirrels are busy.'
'Thank you for coming.'
'What do you want?'
'20 Marlboro Lights.'

'Oil below $50 a barrel?
I feel a complete idiot'

Hybrid Cars

'I rub the balloon on my jumper and the static electricity powers the car'

MORE HYBRID CARS

Shoe thrown at Bush

And finally . . .

'Do you want to buy David Cameron's bike? It comes with a chauffeur-driven car 100 yards behind it'

'Dear Homeowner, I'm pleased to tell you that your rubbish has been offered a place at our council tip...'

'It may be too runny.
Vladimir Putin switched off
the gas while it was cooking'

And finally . . . .

And finally ...

'This protest would be a lot better if we hired some French demonstrators'

'When I was your age I had a train set in my bedroom'

'Good evening,
welcome to ITV'

'He's been specially bred
for his idealism'

And finally . . . .

And finally . . .

'Wearing socks with sandals is enough of a crime to justify taking a DNA sample'

'I'm going to put this DNA sample on our database'

'No, Sarge, this time we're arresting him for incorrect use of apostrophes'

Metric martyrs

'Do you have to do that stupid roaring? This isn't the centre court at Wimbledon'

And finally . . .

'You choose the hospital,
you choose the surgeon
and you choose the
post-operative infection'

'There is a side-effect with
this new drug – the NHS
goes bankrupt'

'Would you like a bar of
chocolate for just £1
with those?'

'Lady in Red...'

And finally . . .

And finally . . .

And finally . . .

And finally …

'*I thought the tear gas was a nice authentic touch*'

Riots in Greece

'*Would you dress up as a judge and award me £60,000? It's one of my fantasies*'

Lurid details emerge

'It's so annoying. I've had that catchy condom jingle on my brain all day'

'Apparently, everyone who has bought a car this year could fit inside one of these'

And finally . . .

Gurkha row

'It's the security services. If you're looking for your glasses they're beside the sink'

CCTV Britain

'Look! The smokers are out early this year'

And finally . . .

'We know you're upset, Dad, but please, please, please don't start dancing'

'Jeremy's been seeing a tutor to prepare him for having his name pulled out of a hat'

Entrance exams abolished

And finally . . .

'It's too early to say how it started, but it will probably turn out to be Gordon Brown's fault'

New statue for Kent

And finally . . .

'How much anti-wrinkle
cream did you use?'